CONNECT
GROW
SERVE
GO

*Moving Toward a Balanced
Approach to an Adult Ministry*

BRET ROBBE
with Dwayne McCrary

LifeWay Press®
Nashville, Tennessee

Connect, Grow, Serve, Go is a heart message for **Bret Robbe**—director of LifeWay's Leadership and Adult Publishing—especially when he sees the lightbulb come on among adult leaders. Before coming to LifeWay Christian Resources in 2006, Bret served churches in Tennessee and Kentucky as pastor.

Bret leads the publishing area that produces all resources for adults in Sunday School; discipleship; magazines/devotionals; and undated studies. As such, he has the joy of hearing how resources contribute to spiritual growth in individuals and in churches—and the privilege of helping meet their ministry needs in the future.

Bret received a D.Min. from The Southern Baptist Theological Seminary in Louisville, Kentucky, and is working toward an M.B.A. degree. He and his wife, Judy (also an educator) have two daughters and live in Franklin, Tennessee.

Dwayne McCrary, a 23-year veteran in educational ministry and a coworker with Bret, helped communicate the ministry experiences and implications of this resource. An editorial project leader, Dwayne has a D.Ed.Min. from New Orleans Baptist Theological Seminary. He and his wife, Lisa, have two children and live in Murfreesboro, Tennessee.

© 2010 LifeWay Press®

Permission is granted to photocopy this resource. A downloadable version is available at *www.lifeway.com*. Additional material not included in the print version is also available for free download at that Web site, including Webcourses, PowerPoint® presentations, and handouts.

ISBN 978-1-4158-6708-2 • Item 005189416

Dewey decimal classification: 259
Subject headings: CHURCH WORK WITH ADULTS \ MINISTRY

This book is a resource for credit in the Christian Growth Study Plan. For information, please visit *www.lifeway.com/CGSP*.

All Scripture quotations are taken from the Holman Christian Standard Bible®, copyright © 1999, 2000, 2001, 2002, 2003 by Holman Bible Publishers. Used by permission.

Printed in the United States of America

Leadership and Adult Publishing; LifeWay Church Resources;
One LifeWay Plaza; Nashville, TN 37234-0175

CONTENTS

Getting Started:
Balance, Moving Forward, and Strategy.................4

Chapter 1 • Connect...................10

Chapter 2 • Grow......................18

Chapter 3 • Serve.....................28

Chapter 4 • Go 36

Next Steps...................................43

Getting Started
Balance, Moving Forward, and Strategy

Cindy loves her church, especially her Bible study groups. She attends one on Sundays and the other, a women's study, on Tuesdays. Both groups feed and challenge her spiritually. Anyone with a question about the Bible turns to Cindy. But things are getting stale for her. A friend gave her some books on doctrine and spiritual truths; Cindy thought if she went deeper into the Word that would lift her out of her spiritual slump. Yet, something still seemed to be missing.

Ken is a pastor seeking God's direction for his church. He wishes they could get some spiritual momentum. The church has this goal, which is printed on worship bulletins and banners and is featured on their Web site: *To know Christ and to make Him known in downtown and beyond.* Lots of activities help people know Christ or make Him known; but planning is reactionary, swinging from one focus to another. The church has no real plan for making their goal happen.

Both Ken and Cindy are looking for something. What they don't realize is they are both looking for the same thing. Both need spiritual focus; one as a church and one as a person. They need something that gives them spiritual balance, something that is simple yet biblical. They want to take action, but they don't know where to start.

If you were one of Ken or Cindy's friends, what would you encourage your friend to do?

Many Christians, churches, and church groups find themselves in the same place. Things seem OK but actually are not quite what they should be. The experience is a lot like driving a car with an out-of-balance tire. When you drive slowly everything feels fine, but when you get up to speed, the ride gets rough. The solution is to either drive slowly all the time or get that tire balanced.

As believers and churches, God created us to move forward, advancing for His glory. When one area of life is out of balance (or worse, missing completely), we can't move forward very well.

Ken and Cindy Moving Forward

Ken's first step was to invite people to pray with him about the church's direction. Some were church leaders while others were active members … like Cindy. The first action the group took was to determine what they wanted to see happen in their own lives. They developed a list of characteristics that might define a thriving Christian and tried to organize their list into four groups. They looked at how the four groupings related to their church goal. They ended up with two items that defined knowing Christ and two that helped make Him known.

If you had been part of this group, what characteristics would you have listed? How would you categorize them?

Ken's church discovered that, at times, they seemed to focus on knowing Christ and then neglect making Him known. As they adjusted, they might then overlook efforts related to helping people know Christ. The characteristics they identified enabled this church to plan with greater intentionality and balance. Now, people are beginning to realize their goal of knowing Christ and making Him known.

As Cindy went though this process she began to understand what was missing in her own life. No question, she was solid in the Word; she realized that to stay spiritually healthy she needed to start giving away what she has learned. She heard about an opportunity to serve in third-grade Sunday School and began investing in the kids. She develops relationships with the parents, too; if they are not believers, she takes every opportunity to share Christ with them. Now Cindy has opportunities to use the evangelism training her pastor taught recently.

Cindy is still involved in her women's group so she can continue to learn God's Word for herself. But now, Cindy is moving forward in her Christian life. She has discovered the balance she needs.

Grouping items into categories gives everyone a better grasp of key elements. The categories of **Connect, Grow, Serve, Go** can help us better understand core elements of the balanced Christian life.

Connect uplifts the importance of worship, prayer, and fellowship in our everyday lives. Connect means to be in vital relationship with God, other believers, the church, and our family. It reminds us of the priority of building positive, long-lasting relationships with people at work, in the school and community, and at home.

As we connect first with God, He makes it possible for us to build meaningful relationships with other believers; they, in turn, help us connect to a church family. These interconnected relationships enable us to welcome people who are not yet part of our church or who are pre-believers.

Grow means knowing and obeying God's Word and understanding how it makes a daily difference in our lives. Gaining knowledge is vital, but we need more than information. True discipleship means discovering something fresh and inspiring in a passage we have read hundreds of times—and acting to apply it.

Serve reminds us of our responsibility to work alongside fellow believers. Our churches are full of ministry and service opportunities—from manning a food pantry to hosting a youth fellowship to teaching Sunday School classes. Every believer working together is required for a local church to function as God intended. God gifts and empowers us to serve and multiplies our efforts in exponential ways.

Go moves us outside the walls of the church and into our community and world. It may mean we drive a nail into a Habitat home, offer a cup of cold water, or tutor a child at an after-school program. It means we develop relationships and discern when it is time to talk about spiritual matters. Going is fed by a desire to experience firsthand God's work in the lives of others, recognizing we are one instrument He is using. **Go** is different from **Serve;** Go is outside the church while Serve is inside.

Adult Ministry Strategy

CONNECT
with an Open Heart
Mark 12:29-31

GO
with
Ready
Feet
Matthew 28:19-20

GROW
in Body,
Mind
& Spirit
Romans 12:2

SERVE
with Willing Hands
1 Peter 4:10-11

A Framework for Dreaming

Connect, Grow, Serve, Go also sets a course—a strategy—for adult ministry. If these four areas represent what defines a thriving and healthy Christian—a believer who is worthy of imitation (1 Cor. 11:1)—then it makes sense that a church must actively seek to develop its people in all four areas.

Every church has some type of strategy, which can be described simply as a plan for obtaining a specific goal or result. Most people in your class or group will tell you they believe their church has a goal of some type. It may be as simple as *reaching our city for Christ* or *making a difference in the lives of people*. The real issue, as was the case with Ken's church, is having a plan to reach your goals, regardless of whether the goal is stated or assumed.

Clues are all around as to what your church is trying to accomplish. For example, the ministries funded by your budget reflect ministries that are important to your church. When you add all the things that are budgeted, you get the big picture of what your church is trying to do.

Every church member is an individual but also an extension of your church. Each member impacts what the church is about in the world while the church as a body impacts individual believers.

Connect, Grow, Serve, Go provides a framework to plan for and think strategically about adult ministry.

A Dynamic Process

Now imagine that when Cindy began to teach, she dropped out of everything else. She attends worship only if the demands of class are not too much; usually you find her in the classroom getting ready.

> **What would you say about her spiritual health now? Is she balanced?**

Just as it is unhealthy to only take in and absorb God's Word, so is it unhealthy to miss out on worship, lose connections with other believers, or stop growing in personal understandings of the Scriptures. If these things happen, the church has failed Cindy by not having a plan—a strategy—in place that helps her maintain spiritual balance. Generally, in Cindy's life, Connect, Grow, Serve, Go all happened within the same time frame. She did not get connected, then start to grow in order to serve, and then begin to go. This process will happen in different ways for every believer. Too many dynamics are at work to say that all four things must happen in a certain order. Our personal needs, relationships, life situations, and mentor networks all play a part in how we begin and move forward in our spiritual growth. The issue is not when each part of the process happens but that each one does occur.

Having said all this, we move to the million-dollar question:

How do we foster each area of Connect, Grow, Serve, Go in a balanced way?

The remainder of this resource is designed to give you ideas and suggestions to make this balance happen in your church and in individual believers. You will find stories to help you recognize how Connect, Grow, Serve, Go works and begin to think about how it can happen in your church, class or group, and your own life.

Our goal is clear: to help you and your church become balanced in its ministry to adults.

1
CONNECT
with an Open Heart

" 'This is the most important,' Jesus answered:
'Listen, Israel! The Lord our God, The Lord is One.
Love the Lord your God with all your heart, with
all your soul, with all your mind, and with all your
strength. The second is: Love your neighbor as
yourself. There is no other commandment greater
than these.' " *Mark 12:29-31*

Great groups and thriving Christians encourage a deepening relationship with God and relationships of integrity with other people.

People Need Relationships

Approximately three years ago, Rick and Jan moved to a new community and their lives quickly changed. Jan became a stay-at-home wife and Rick jumped into a pressure-filled job. Jan needed to talk and Rick needed to work. Jan fell into a deep depression after a miscarriage. Their marriage was crumbling and they were on the verge of divorce.

One day a woman at the gym invited Jan to attend church with her. She accepted the invitation and Rick went along for the ride. They found themselves at church on Mother's Day, a very hard day for people who have faced a miscarriage. Rick felt as if everyone around him knew he didn't want to be there. But that soon changed.

The people this couple met were honest and real. They seemed to have the same type of issues Jan and Rick did. The turning point came when this couple got involved in a group for people who were about their same age and going through the same type of family struggles.

"We had so many people praying for us that despite fighting hard against it," Rick said, "I didn't have a chance. I recommitted my life to Christ and felt reborn. I want to help others get connected, too."

From this couple's story some key principles stand out:
- Rick and Jan were at a breaking point and were searching for hope.
- They needed relationships built on trust and honesty.
- Someone cared enough to invite them to be part of a group that fellowships and worships God together.
- Jan and Rick found real people who truly care about them.
- People sincerely prayed for them. We can seek to establish honest relationships, but only God can change people's lives.

Removing Barriers

Did you notice that Rick and Jan connected with God, with others in a group, with the church body, and with each other? First, they got connected to God. Notice what Rick said; he recommitted his life to Christ and felt reborn. At one time, he had made a commitment to Christ but apparently had not invested in that relationship. Rick began to rediscover that relationship by being a part of worship. He admitted that it felt awkward at first.

Think for a moment about the people who will attend your church, class, or group for the first time in the next six weeks. Put yourself in their places. Think of the questions they may have as they come that first time. *Will I know what to do? Who will talk to me? What if they ask me about something I don't want to talk about? What if I am not accepted? How will I know where to go? Who will take care of my children?* The list could go on. The questions they raise are the issues of **Connect.**

Every church and class has a "code" or culture of some kind. It may be that everyone stands when the Bible is read, wears a name tag, or finds the Scripture reference printed on a marker board before class begins. These examples reflect unwritten expectations that are assumed by regular attenders. Knowing the code means you are "in."

Nothing is wrong with codes as long as they don't interfere with new people being able to connect. One thing we can do as a group and as individuals is to identify those unknown codes and look for newcomers whom we can help assimilate. In most cases, all we need to do is help them find the Bible passage, show them where to go, and help them know when to stand or sit. This assistance may be an organized effort or just reflect someone seeing a need and responding to it.

Connecting with God in Worship

The first order of business for Rick and Jan was to build their relationship with God and, appropriately so, since this relationship impacts all others. Jesus reminded His hearers that if they were disconnected from Him, they would be incapable of doing anything productive (John 15:4-5).

Worship is all about Him. You may wonder what you can offer in worship—you don't sing, preach, or take up the offering. You would not be the first person to feel that way.

At one time, Beau had similar thoughts. He complained that he wasn't getting anything out of corporate worship. He attended regularly, took diligent notes, and still seemed to be walking away with nothing. When asked what he was contributing to worship, he admitted he was there as a taker, looking for something to happen to him not by him.

Beau felt challenged to give personally to the worship service. He was self-conscious about singing and, as a college student, had time and money issues. The best thing he felt he could give was prayer.

He committed to pray for each person leading the service, that God would give them clear minds as they led, shared a testimony, or presented a sermon. Worship began to come alive for Beau. He realized God was at work, and his prayers began to change from "help them" to "thank You for helping them." His worship became ongoing conversation with God as he saw God work in and through prayer. His prayer helped create the caring community that Rick and Jan discovered when they began to attend.

Unfortunately, many people think of worship the same way Beau once did—as something to be observed with the hope of getting something out of it. True worship grows out of participation. Each of us must find a way to participate, to give back through worship. Our spiritual health demands that we Connect in worship.

Can you relate to Beau's initial feelings about being disconnected during worship? If so, in what ways?

How does your church encourage participation in worship? In what ways are you taking advantage of those opportunities?

How can you follow Beau's example to become more active in your worship of God?

As a term, worship can be difficult to define but easier to spot. In simple terms, worship is the response that occurs when a person recognizes greatness. For Christians, worship is our heartfelt response of praise and adoration to God, to His revealing Himself, to His greatness and glory. We bow in awe, in repentance, and in submission to God. We share with Him about His importance in our lives and listen to Him through prayer.

Worship is a primary connecting point with God as we declare His greatness, our enjoyment of His blessings, and our obedience to His direction. Our relationship with God develops as we respond in worship to His activity in our lives. And when believers worship together, they share a bond unlike any other.

Connecting and Reconnecting with Family

Rick and Jan could not be the husband and wife they needed to be if they were disconnected from God. Finding a connection with God was just the start. Remember, their marriage was in trouble. Jan was hurting from a move and a miscarriage. Rick was stressed beyond his limits. And both were in a town full of strangers. Before they could build other relationships, they needed to take care of their marriage.

Many of us are damaged from our past and the hardships of life. Deaths, failures, and disappointments all contribute to the sense of being burdened. Jan and Rick attended a marriage retreat planned for young

Getting Some Culture

As she makes contact with the parents in her class, Lisa is being exposed to different cultures. Not all of them have grown up in a church, and some have strange ideas about God. Most had gotten their ideas from television preachers or religious guru blogs. Lisa began to read some books by the names that kept coming up so she could put together a response.

One family Lisa visited almost didn't let her in the house. One of her preschoolers had a birthday and she wanted to give him a book. Her husband had just gotten home from work so he wore his work clothes. His job required him to wear dark slacks and a dark tie. He happened to be wearing a white shirt as well.

When the mom looked out the peephole, all she could see was Lisa's husband and assumed Mormon missionaries were visiting the home. When she looked through the hole a second time, Lisa had moved so she could be seen too. The mom immediately recognized her and opened the door. Everyone got a good laugh as the mom told Lisa and her husband who she thought they were.

Lisa learned an important lesson about details that day. Now she makes her husband wear a golf shirt when she takes him along. She also stands in front of her husband to make sure she is the one seen if people look through a peephole. She is doing all she can to make sure she builds bridges to others as she goes in Christ's name.

Going on Purpose

As Lisa listened to her training partners tell about sharing with their friends, she realized all her friends were churched. As she thought about it, she had very little contact with unchurched people, even at work. She realized that if she wasn't around lost people she would never lead anyone to Christ. Lisa begin to look for natural ways to build relationships with lost people.

She became the team mom for her son's baseball team. She enlisted as a sponsor for trips taken by her daughter's basketball team. Both teams were begging for volunteers so why not her?

As she travels with the basketball team, works concession stands with other parents, and sits in the stands watching ball games, she gets to talk to unchurched people. They talk about raising children,

When the other leader in her class asked her to be one of her partners in the evangelism plan their church was putting together, it was just what she was looking for—to be held accountable by someone. The plan the church was using gave her that accountability. Every week, someone would go with her to make contacts, as well as ask her about the natural opportunities she had during the week to share. She knew that several parents of the kids she taught were not believers.

We all need to be held accountable to those things we should be doing. This accountability could be formal, as it was in Lisa's church, or informal, with Christian friends being responsible to each other. Either way will work, as long as people are holding each other accountable for sharing as they go.

Training with Accountability Is a Good Start

The training Lisa chose to attend began each week with each participant sharing with a partner about opportunities since the last meeting to share Jesus. For most, this share time was the best part of the training. Lisa and her co-teacher visited all the parents of the children in their Sunday School class and talked to each one about their spiritual lives. They already knew most of these parents, but this visit only made them better preschool teachers. They discovered needs they were unaware of and began to find ways to meet those needs.

During the training Lisa really didn't learn anything she hadn't already heard. The group reviewed some very familiar Bible passages and revisited many of the basic teachings about salvation. The difference came in how the material was organized. Everyone memorized a plan for sharing, which helped Lisa get a handle on sharing the familiar information. Having a plan gave her confidence. She didn't always use the plan exactly as she memorized it, but it was there if she needed it.

The church continues to provide training for people wanting to improve as a witness. Not everyone takes advantage of this opportunity. Some feel they already know how to share the gospel and see no need to get more training. For Lisa, the training helped her become aware of her need to continue to develop. Every time she shares with someone, she learns something new about herself and is introduced to more questions she needed to process. The training helps her stay sharp and learn new ways to share her faith.

Even though Lisa found it easy to talk to people, she was really shy at heart. She had been voted "most shy" by her high school senior class and she continued to carry that title into her adult life. It was a lot easier to just invite people to attend a women's Bible study with her than to be the actual person who shared with her friends about Jesus.

All this hesitancy was about to change. Every Sunday School class was asked to participate in the evangelism training provided by her church. She and another preschool teacher signed up. She was apprehensive but hopeful that she would finally be able to move beyond her shyness and begin to talk to others about Jesus.

We Know We Should

Brush your teeth. Wash your hands. Eat all your veggies. Take your vitamins. Get an annual physical. These are all things we know we should do but sometimes forget or delay. We know these things are important but often hear the message so much that we ignore it or become complacent.

Many Christians could add an item to this list: *Share Jesus with everyone.* Just like Lisa, we know we are supposed to be telling others about Jesus. We learned about Him because someone told us, so it makes sense that we are expected to do the same. We can't read the four Gospels without finding it—from "I will make you fish for people" (Matt. 4:19) to "Go … and make disciples of all nations" (Matt. 28:19). You really can't miss it.

Since it is obvious that we are to be telling others about Jesus, why don't we? For Lisa, it was a matter of motivation. She had all she really wanted. Her relationship with God was strong. She had plenty of Christian friends and was active in the women's ministry of her church. She had a place of service where she was finding a great deal of affirmation and encouragement. Her children had already made commitments to Christ. By most accounts, she was a fulfilled Christian.

The only problem was that she lived with guilt for not sharing Jesus with others. It was beginning to cause her to doubt her salvation. She wondered: *If we tell others about those we love and I am not telling others about Jesus, does that mean I really am not a true believer?*

She couldn't tell anyone about her questions because everyone thought she "had it all together." To admit her struggle to anyone would only destroy the expectations she felt others had of her. So it was better just to sit in silence.

Great groups and thriving Christians engage in disciple-making that is based in compassion, obedience, and prayer.

The One Missing Thing

Lisa grew up in the church and accepted Christ when she was young. She had a great foundation of Bible knowledge and was always involved in worship. Her prayer life and devotional life were vital parts of her everyday discipleship. She was one of the Preschool Sunday School teachers every parent wanted their children to experience. She cared for the children in her class as if they were her own. She had the respect of everyone in her church.

Only one thing was missing ... she was not an active witness for Christ. She had heard about the need for witnessing all her life, but it just wasn't for her.

4

GO
with Ready Feet

"Go, therefore, and make disciples of all nations,
baptizing them in the name of the Father and
of the Son and of the Holy Spirit, teaching them
to observe everything I have commanded you.
And remember, I am with you always, to the end
of the age." *Matthew 28:19-20*

On the classroom wall are pictures of those who "have been sent out" (Go) from the class to do ministry in other areas of the church. Often during prayer time, the class prays for the ministry of these people. They are never forgotten, and every class member knows that he too needs to be open to being called by God to do ministry in other places. A culture of Serve is ingrained in the hearts and lives of class members.

Every year, Sonny has a big Thanksgiving class party and invites every current and former class member. It has become the largest event the church plans each year. Everyone shares a meal together and tells how they have seen God work through them in the past year. Then they head to the local homeless shelter to prepare the meals that will be served on Thanksgiving … serving, always serving.

What is your church or group doing to help people find a place to serve?

How can your church or group help you learn to use your gifts more effectively?

How can you follow the example of Sonny and the other members of his class?

Did you think about ...

Responding to a call to short-term or full-time missions?

Agreeing to serve as a deacon or an usher?

Leading home groups in your community?

Working in your church's welcome center?

Singing in the adult choir?

Joining a ministry team/church committee?

Serving your community (food pantries, construction projects, clothes closets, and so forth)?

Using your gifts in church media and public relations projects?

The church becomes more effective as Connect, Grow, Serve, Go all work together. Serving gives depth to Bible study (Grow) as members and guests look for ways to apply what they are learning. Service is a natural outcome of relationships (Connect). Relationships would be empty if no one ever responded to the needs that are expressed between friends.

Serving alongside others also strengthens the connections a person already has. The sense of being part of a team emerges. In many cases, service leads to opportunities for sharing our faith with others. Such ministry can be the vehicle that gives us credibility and a willing ear.

One More Thing

We need to tell you one more thing about Sonny's class. It is not the largest in the church because he sends people out who are capable and willing to serve in other areas. That doesn't kill his class; it builds it. Every time someone is sent out of the class a chair opens up for a person not yet reached. A new person will fill that seat and the process begins all over again. That adds life both to the class and to the church.

Start the Conversation

Applying Serve

1. Think about all the ways a person could serve through a Sunday School class. Here is a list to get you started:

Teacher	Care-group leader
Teacher apprentice	Records keeper
Prayer coordinator	Prayer warrior
Greeter	Coffee maker
Room cleaner	Chair arranger
Announcement maker	Party planner
Outreach team member	Ministry project planner

Class Facebook® group host
(or other Internet community services)

How does Sonny's Sunday School story generate ideas for serving in other areas of your church and community? List as many ideas as you can.

In those conversations, Allen draws on what he has learned and is learning. His growing knowledge of the Bible is helping him reach his friends for Jesus Christ (**Go**).

The biggest thing going on in Allen's life relates to his family. His ex-wife was skeptical at first, but she brings their children to Sunday School. She had wanted that so much when they were married and now it is happening. She began attending a women's Sunday School class. As Allen studied the Bible, he became aware of things he had done wrong as a husband and father.

He and his former wife are talking and are trying to put their marriage back together. They know the odds are against them, but with God's help and the support they are finding in their Sunday School classes and other groups, they think they can make it work this time.

Allen's story is extreme is some ways, but it doesn't have to be.

> **How many "Allens" do you think live within 15 miles of your church? How many do you know personally?**

"Allens," with great stories about how the Bible has changed their lives, are all around us. If we are honest, we will admit we need to be challenged to continue to Grow. The opportunity to study the Bible with others is a gift from God, one we should nurture and use.

Start the Conversation

Applying Grow

Jesus drove His followers to two things: Himself and His words. In a time of great religious turmoil, it is easy to choose style over substance, ritual over spiritual growth. Christian growth has more to do with transformation than with raw numbers. God has a metamorphosis in mind for His people—one that will result in lives that are constantly thriving in their faith.

1. In Romans 12, Paul called for a change in how a person lives. Regardless of what kind of change is necessary, it is born out of personal interactions with God.

   If your church or group had been featured in this book, what would we be reading about? How would your church or group be a positive example?

   What opportunities does your church or group provide for you to continue to grow?

   If we were following your life instead of Allen's, how would this story read? What are you doing to grow in knowing, understanding, and living out the truths of the Bible?

2. "Participate" in the following conversation of an after-church meeting with adult leaders. Complete it based on what you are learning about Connect, Grow, Serve, Go and your own group's needs and opportunities. You may also want to visit *www.lifeway. com/curriculumguide* to discover resources that can feed into this conversation and other discussions.

"Thanks for taking the time to meet briefly, everyone," Guy welcomed. "We do need to touch base on a few things. So, John, start us off."

"Sure, Guy. I had the privilege of coordinating the first Habitat for Humanity® project. It seems as if more and more people who eventually become members of our church are introduced to us by some type of community project. Allen is a great example. I'm glad we want to continue offering these opportunities—as well as new Bible study groups. It's a draw that appeals to people who want to make a difference somehow in the world. And Allen has certainly made a difference in our church."

"I agree, John," Mary said. "I think we contributed to his spiritual journey, and he has energized and taught us a lot about faith, too—especially when it comes to inviting friends. Many in our community who may come, will not have any church background but do have an opinion about spiritual things. We discovered that in Adult VBS last year—with a lot of lively, spirited discussion! Some opinions may seem to be a hodgepodge of ideas, but they are opinions. If we show respect and listen, hopefully people will keep the door open."

"And I have become convinced that many people have strong commitments to spiritual growth and simply need encouragement," John added. "Some people in our church have been believers a long time. Some have all the facts, but little apparent change in their lives. What are some ways we can help them? I can't wait to hear your ideas!"

If you had been at this meeting with Guy, John, and Mary, what suggestions would you offer to help members of this church?

3
SERVE
with Willing Hands

"Based on the gift they have received, everyone should use it to serve others, as good managers of the varied grace of God. … If anyone serves, his service should be from the strength God provides, so that in everything God may be glorified through Jesus Christ. To Him belong the glory and the power forever and ever." *1 Peter 4:10-11*

Great groups and thriving Christians embrace a lifestyle of focused ministry, serving others out of their spiritual giftedness and mutual encouragement.

One Man Cared Enough

Sonny teaches a Sunday School class that holds a unique honor. Other classes are larger, and others have better Bible study leaders (Sonny will be the first to tell you that). But here is where his class stands out.

If you were to visit every Sunday School class in this church, you will find at least one worker who at one time was part of Sonny's class. They were not displeased with Sonny or the class. In fact, they are doing what they are doing because Sonny prepared them to do it. Half of the church's greeters are or were in Sonny's class, too!

Sonny wants to see how many people he can prepare to serve in the church, and he is doing it through how he leads his Sunday School class.

In Sonny's class, everyone has a job to do. He tries to match people with their gifts and desires. The people who are organizers plan the class parties and ministry projects. The people who have the gift of hospitality greet everyone and host guests. The people with the gift of evangelism or shepherding follow up with every guest. Those with the gift of mercy keep up with those who are facing physical or emotional struggles. Sonny even has one person who has the gift of service and straightens up the room after class is over. Everybody is doing something and is being affirmed for it.

Not long ago a couple were guests in Sonny's class. When they arrived, they were greeted by a regular attendee and they began to get to know each other. As other class members arrived, the person who had greeted the couple introduced them and pointed out interests each class member had in common with the guests.

Another class member offered a cup of fresh coffee he had made that morning. The guests were gracious but declined. When asked whether they would like some water instead, they agreed and the class member left the room, returning with two cups full of cold water.

At the end of class, a care leader noticed that the guests had written a prayer request on the class prayer sheet (passed around during class for Sonny to review before dismissing). This leader told Sonny that she would contact the wife and get more information about the request.

Early the next week, a team from the class came by and visited the couple. Sonny has discovered that in a world of sitting behind machines, the best way to get to know someone is face-to-face. They visited on the front porch for about 15 minutes. In that time, the team learned that the couple had grown up going to church but both quit when they went to college, where they had met. The team also learned that the care leader had called and prayed with them about the request they had written on the class prayer sheet.

As the team left, the couple said they would be coming back. When asked why, they said everyone was so friendly and caring. The wife added, "One man even cared enough to clean the room after the class was over."

This couple had experienced the power of a team serving together. The fact that the room was cleaned even after the class was over communicated a great deal to this couple. Interestingly, this couple didn't say anything about the actual Bible study. They evaluated the class based on the friendliness, individual care, and respect shown by this team of people. Each part working together had made a greater impact than the actual study itself.

Sonny wants to pursue the goal of spiritually balanced Christians, and he knows that balance includes more than growing in Bible knowledge. Spiritual health includes putting into action those things class members are learning. This action is **Serve.**

Every Job is Important

The service provided by this team highlights some things we all need to remember. First of all, every job is important to the whole. Suppose the man cleaning the room after class had not done his job? Would the guest couple have had the same impression of the class? Maybe, but maybe not. What if the person who found the cups of cold water had ignored the request? How important was his simple gesture in communicating that the class cared? Every person taking care of his or her action was and is important.

The things you do or could be doing are important to the whole. If you are not doing your part, then something is missing. It's like a thousand-piece puzzle with one piece missing. The missing piece goes unnoticed until you look at how it fits with the other pieces. What you do makes a difference to someone.

Every Believer Is Gifted at Something

The second reality we observe from Sonny's class is that people need to serve through their giftedness. If the people who were gifted with hospitality were asked to clean the room, they would be frustrated. If the person who cleaned the room was asked to greet every person (breaking the ice with people he has never met is just not him), both he and the guests would be frustrated.

God gifts every believer with at least one special gift. It is our responsibility to discover it, develop it, and use it to the fullest. To be able to work through our giftedness, we have to know what that gift is. Every person who is a part of Sonny's class has had some time with him going over spiritual gifts and evaluating which one or ones he or she may have.

SERVE

Sonny lets them try different things in the class until they find their place—one that matches their giftedness. He encourages them and double-checks on every class member to see what they are thinking about using their gifts in God's service.

One thing you need to know about Sonny is he doesn't believe his dominant spiritual gift to be that of teaching. He has learned how to teach. His primary gift is service. He views his role as teacher in terms of serving those he teaches. By that he tries to serve those on his class list so that they can better serve and find fulfillment through serving in the church. He declares himself to be a "servant to the serving." He also reminds people that Jesus called Peter to shepherd His sheep (John 21) and that shepherds are servants.

Trained for Success

A third reality we observe from Sonny and his class of servants is that training made a difference in some way. The things that happened on the day the guests arrived happened because each person had been trained to do the task. Sonny and others had helped them understand how to be a success.

Along with that training comes helping people see the possibilities. Remember the class member who cleans the room? He had been frustrated for a long time trying to find a way to serve. The coffee making was already assigned and the room was already set up. There was nothing left for him to do. So there he sat.

However, the church began to grow and a second Sunday School hour was added. The class that Sonny uses gets used by a different class later in the morning. On the first Sunday that this new class began to use the room, a church janitor came through picking up trash.

Sonny immediately recognized that this situation represented a new job and asked this man if he could take on that work. He jumped at the opportunity. He had finally found a place to serve.

couples which was a real help. They reconnected with each other and now are beginning to have a marriage worth imitating. It took some honesty and real work by both of them, but it was worth it.

Prior to getting things worked out, they were sour and needy. People with whom they had tried to build a relationship pulled away. Friends didn't mind listening to Rick or Jan, but they didn't want the relationship to be a constant gripe session. Now those same people see something in Rick and Jan that makes them want to be around them. In this light, Connect reflects spiritual health and balance.

Jan got help by attending a support group for women who have had miscarriages. Just knowing other women were feeling the same emotions was important. As she dealt with her feelings she became a better wife—and hopefully would be a good mom if God saw fit for this to happen in the future.

Jesus modeled such ministry and personal connections as He related to people throughout His earthly ministry. The early church met daily and cared for one another's needs with consistency. When a church today has a plan like Connect, Grow, Serve, Go, these are the types of ministries that strategically lead to helping people become spiritually healthy believers.

Connecting with Friends

Let's be honest. Regardless of where we live or how long we have lived there, we need relationships. Rick and Jan needed some friends. They found them in their Bible study class. It didn't happen overnight, but it did happen. As they became involved in other groups, their circle of friends grew.

Rick is now helping other people "get connected," as he puts it. He remembers what it is like to be on the outside. His desire to help others get connected is growing into something more—into telling others about Christ. Rick cannot help but tell others about the God who gives Him life and purpose.

Connect and Grow, Serve, Go

Being connected with God in a personal and vital way, as Rick's growth illustrates, motivates and even compels us to tell others about it.

Gary and Joan are in love with each other. They have been married almost 40 years but still go on dates. Even though she knows they will go out every Thursday night, Gary still calls her and asks her if she wants to go out that night. Then he'll brag the next day about where they ate, what movie they saw, and where they went. He doesn't mean to brag about Joan to his friends, but he just cannot help himself.

That's the way it is when we are vitally connected to God. We just can't help ourselves.

Remember Beau? He enjoyed his prayer ministry so much that he invited some friends to participate with him. They began to write notes to the people who led the service, thanking them for their willingness and commitment. They asked for the names of choir members so they could pray for them as well. In time, they received information on people the pastor was aware needed prayer. They may have only had a first name or initials, but they prayed for God to work in that unknown person's life during worship. Now they are not only worshiping through prayer, they also are serving through prayer as well.

Through their experience of prayer in worship, Beau's friends are asking about prayer and fasting. They have sought some help and the church is providing an eight-week Bible study about the prayer life of Jesus. Beau and his friends want to grow in their understanding of prayer so they can do it better and more effectively.

Start the Conversation

Applying Connect

Rick thought everyone was so helpful and friendly that first day he and Jan attended their church. One person in particular helped him find everything. Rick didn't know it, but this lady does the same thing every week. She looks for people she doesn't know with the hope of finding a first-time guest to help. This church is intentional about making sure everyone in attendance connects with someone in some way.

What are some intentional things your church and groups in your church do to help people connect with others?

How do they help guests make those initial connections?

What is your church doing to help people worship?

What resources are being provided that encourage personal worship?

What is your church or group doing to help people deal with life's hurts and changes?

What is your group doing to build stronger relationships within the group?

How does your church and the groups in which you participate encourage prayer?

2
GROW
in Body, Mind, and Spirit

"Do not be conformed to this age, but be
transformed by the renewing of your mind, so
that you may discern what is the good, pleasing,
and perfect will of God." *Romans 12:2*

Great groups and thriving
Christians explore God's
Word with other believers,
participating in the life
change that results from
believing and obeying God.

God's Word Changes Everything

A ministry team at the church had taken on a Habitat for Humanity®
project. The church was challenged to supply all the labor on this
project while local businesses helped fund the work.

Two ministry team members invited a mutual friend, Allen, to
join them. Allen was looking for a way to be more involved in the
community and he loved construction work, so he accepted. As he and
the others worked on the house, friendships developed and, in due time,
spiritual matters became a topic of discussion. Allen didn't grow up
going to church but was interested. Eventually, he committed his life
to Christ. He began attending worship services at the church, bringing
his unchurched friends with him. He didn't know a lot, but what he did
know he shared with his friends as best he could.

All this Bible stuff was new to him. He had no idea how to find a Bible reference. Everyone around him seemed to do it with ease and he was doing all he could to use the contents page. His unchurched friends had all kinds of questions about the Bible and he was the only person they knew who was attending a church.

Allen wanted to learn more and knew he would have to do more than listen to a sermon one time a week. He shared his desire with one of the men who had invited him in the first place. This friend told him about a small-group Bible study that he attended every Sunday. Allen eagerly accompanied his friend the next week with a strong desire to discover answers to his other friends' questions as well as some of his own.

Allen had friends in the church, was involved in service through the church's construction team, and was sharing with others about Jesus as best he could. But Allen knew he needed to grow in his knowledge and understanding of the Bible.

We Need Nutrition to Grow

To grow physically, we need food—the right kind of food. We may love vanilla ice cream. But if that were the only thing we ate, we would soon be in trouble physically. We need something more than just vanilla ice cream—like chocolate syrup, almond slivers, and cherries!

What we allow ourselves to eat is important to our spiritual health as well. Paul stated it this way: "Brothers, by the mercies of God, I urge you to present your bodies as a living sacrifice, holy and pleasing to God; this is your spiritual worship. Do not be conformed to this age, but be transformed by the renewing of your mind, so that you may discern what is the good, pleasing, and perfect will of God" (Rom. 12:1-2).

We need nutrition and it needs to be balanced. Connect, Serve, and Go without Grow will leave us spiritually malnourished.

Open Groups Planned for All

The group that Allen was invited to attend was a Sunday School class—considered an open group because members expect guests every week. The class Allen attended was for both men and women. He could have attended other classes, but this was where his friends were.

When he arrived, he was greeted by a teacher who was friendly and helpful. Allen's friend had already told the teacher Allen would be coming, so the teacher was ready. Allen was given the book they were using to help with their Bible study. The first page of the lesson had a paperclip so Allen could easily find it. His friend helped Allen find the Bible passage.

As other class members entered the room, Allen recognized many of them from the Habitat project. That helped him feel more at ease. The teacher didn't waste much time getting into the Bible study. Allen soon realized that the question on a marker board was there for a purpose. A lot of discussion and interaction about the Bible passage occurred.

Allen wanted to ask lots of things, but on this first day he just observed. There was certainly no pressure to get involved, but he didn't feel excluded either.

At one point in the class, someone asked a question from the Bible chapter being studied. It was one of the questions Allen had wondered about, too. He was amazed as the group wrestled with an answer. Different opinions were expressed, not all of them in agreement. The teacher asked more questions to help everyone get a better picture of some of the issues they needed to consider on the topic.

To Allen's surprise, no one seemed to feel belittled or minimized for disagreeing; instead, everyone was challenged to examine the Bible passage and compare what he or she understood about the topic. The class even developed a list of other things they needed to think about if they were going to get a clearer understanding.

After class, the teacher made a point to catch Allen and ask him whether he had any questions about the class. Allen wondered whether he could get a copy of the questions the class had listed. The teacher obliged and encouraged Allen to write them in his copy of the book they were using so he could look at them later. That's when Allen realized the book was his to keep. The teacher then showed Allen how to use the book and what to do before the next session if he chose.

Allen went home that afternoon and read the material about the previous week's studies. He wanted to catch up if he could, even though doing so was not required. As he read the lesson for the next week, he wrote down his questions. He wasn't going to ask all of them, but he was going to ask at least one of them to "test the waters." He wanted to make sure he would get treated with the same kind of respect he had witnessed that first Sunday.

Healthy Christian growth includes exploring God's Word with other believers. Many books of the Bible were originally addressed to groups of people in specific regions. In some instances, books written to individuals were also directed to the people around that individual. For example, Paul's letter to Philemon was also directed to the group of believers who were meeting in Philemon's home.

Although each of us is responsible for our own growth in Christ, we are also accountable to help one another in that growth. Thriving Christians explore God's Word with other believers through study, reflection on the truths discovered, and conversation so that life change can and does take place.

A Plan for Study

Allen's story highlights several things churches can do to help people grow in their knowledge and understanding of the Bible. First, this church had a plan and was following it. The book that was handed to Allen gave some direction to both the teacher and the class. In this church, every adult was studying the same passage. That made it possible for Allen to discuss the lesson with other friends who were attending different classes. That may not happen every week, but at least it was possible.

Having a plan took some pressure off the teacher. Having a plan also meant the class would deal with lessons the teacher might not have selected, giving balance to the class. The truth is most teachers select studies with which they are comfortable or interested. Since every adult was studying the same Bible passage, the pastor could address some of the same themes in his sermons.

The church made sure the teacher had all he needed to be a success by providing him resources that gave him additional ideas. He had access to a room that had supplies (including markers that worked!). The teacher had been trained to lead this class and was being developed through weekly meetings the church offered its teachers.

The church had a plan for growth—not "teach what you want" but one that takes seriously the whole counsel of God's Word and not just the most popular subjects. Allen picked up right away that the Bible was central to helping him grow as a Christian.

A Safe Place to Explore

The church and class placed some important expectations on the teacher as well. The class was to be a place where people could ask questions and study together—not a place to "sit and soak" while one person presents a fact-filled lecture.

This class encourages critical thinking—class members think through what they believe, why they believe it, how those beliefs are impacted by the Bible, and what difference the study makes Monday-Saturday.

These goals make it exciting for both guests and regular attendees. Everyone can participate, but no one is forced to do so. Those who want to study in advance are encouraged to because they can participate in the discussion more fully. At the same time, those who have not done any study before class are not punished or looked down on. They can still ask questions and participate.

Moving Toward Life Change

While gaining knowledge is important, it is not the only thing. This class functions with the hope that there will be a difference in how each person lives. One of the jobs of the teacher is to keep the discussion clearly focused so the group doesn't get sidetracked simply chasing facts and information. They are to be looking for understanding, application, and life change.

One more thing—Allen was divorced and his children live in the same town. Once he found out that Bible studies were available for all ages at the same time, he begin asking his former wife if their children could attend Sunday School at his church. She was blown away. The divorce had occurred because of Allen, and she had seen no other option to protect the spiritual health of herself and her children.

Closed Groups to Dig Deeper

In time, Allen began to be introduced to other kinds of Bible studies in his church. At first, the Sunday School class was providing him all he could take in. But that was starting to change. He wanted to know about some very specific topics in the Bible and began to realize other study groups could help him. These groups were different from the Sunday School class in that once they got started, they didn't allow new people to join them. The class would be offered at a later time and he could join it then.

Allen wanted to know more about how to study the Bible, how to deal with finances, and how to be a good father to his children. His church offered groups that addressed these needs. Some were informal and others were very structured with lots of accountability. The class topic usually determined the structure and level of accountability. Some groups met weekly while others met monthly. Some lasted three weeks while others lasted three months. Once again, it depended on the topic. Allen couldn't do it all, but he could at least do something to go deeper in his Bible knowledge and understanding.

What was offered was not haphazard. Every year, the church took a survey to determine the issues and needs of the people in the church. Sunday School teachers also shared information regarding issues that continued to come up in their classes. While some topics were givens (marriage, parenting, Baptist beliefs), the surveys help church leaders know they are providing the right kinds of groups to meet the needs of the church. In some cases, the church combined with other churches in the area to address a need they were unable to meet alone (these groups always met away from the respective churches).

These kinds of studies are important because they add depth to the ministry of the church. While a Sunday School class is a good first step, not every issue can be addressed in detail every week. Other groups are needed to provide for the depth some of these issues require.

Grow Leads to More

Look at what being a part of these kinds of Bible study groups is doing for Allen. He is discovering the truth of the Bible and is being encouraged to apply it. The expectation of the church, of the Bible study groups, and of Allen is that he will do something with the knowledge he is gaining. He is becoming the person he always wanted but didn't know how to be.

He still helps with Habitat projects but now in a different way. He helps organize Bible studies during the breaks as they work on the site (**Grow**). No one knows why they didn't do it before, but they are glad they are doing it now. They are growing while serving.

Allen has invited some of his friends to work on the site with him. These are the guys he ran around with before he got involved in church. As they work with Allen, they begin to talk about spiritual things (the beginnings of **Connect**).

family traditions, and current events. When appropriate, Lisa brings up spiritual matters as well.

Some parents have begun to seek her out, looking for advice and answers to their spiritual questions. For the first time, she is living out the command to go—and is loving how God is using her to make an eternal difference.

Going Full Circle

At a family reunion, Lisa had the opportunity to talk to a nephew about spiritual things. He was thinking about life, and she was one of several to talk to him. His parents had told him the same things, but it was different coming from his favorite aunt. A couple of weeks later, he called her, inviting her to attend his baptism. He gave her the address and the name of the church where he would be baptized.

Lisa did an Internet search to find out more about the church, and was she ever surprised! A few years ago, her church's youth group had gone on a mission trip to a neighboring county. The teenagers conducted Backyard Bible Clubs in an area that did not have a local church. Their goal was to find people to help start a new church. As a preschool teacher, she went with the youth for a couple of days.

Honestly, she had forgotten about it, but she soon remembered: That group had indeed established a church and, 14 years later, her nephew was going to be baptized in it.

We never know where our going may lead. We don't know what God is up to and how He will use our efforts. We don't know whose nephew may be waiting to be baptized because of our efforts. We don't know what parents may be needing as they watch a baseball game. What we do know is that we are to go and let God do the rest. It may be our nephew who is baptized because we go.

Start the Conversation
Applying Go

1. Scan the stories from Lisa's life that have been included in this chapter. Look for things she did, as well as actions her church and other groups took that made it possible for her to be an effective Go-er. Fill in the three columns on page 42.

Things Lisa Did	Things Her Church/Groups Did	Things Lisa Could Have Done

2. Look for ways becoming a Go-er impacted Lisa's connection to God and other people, challenged her to grow in her knowledge of the Bible, and helped her serve more effectively. Write those ways in the space that follows.

Strengthening CONNECT	*Strengthening* GROW	*Strengthening* SERVE

What can you do as an individual or through the groups you influence that will help you Go to other people with the gospel?

Next Steps
Putting It All Together

Several years ago, a technology company developed a commercial to be viewed during the Super Bowl. One of the scenes featured a cowboy saying "You see the movies, you hear the stories ... I'm living a dream."[1]

In the previous pages, you have experienced stories that define a balanced adult ministry. These stories are from different places and different churches. Some are from rural communities and some are from urban centers. The churches people attend are just like your church— imperfect but trying to make a difference.

What about your church? Is your church providing a balanced ministry that includes each element of Connect, Grow, Serve, Go? How so?

Often, church leaders, when asked about areas in which their church is weak, will offer excuses. Most of the time it is actually because they have been concentrating on areas of strength and not focusing on areas of weakness.

For example, Sam is a pastor. He is preaching the best sermons he can preach every Sunday. He cannot understand why it is so hard to get people to volunteer to serve in the church; yet, when you look at the training offered, all of it is based in Connect and Grow.

Sam has been doing a great job preaching and leading his church; until now, though, he had not made the connection that he was not teaching his people to Serve and Go. Although he mentions these things in his sermons, not one discipleship class has been offered to teach his people how to Serve and Go.

How is your understanding of Connect, Grow, Serve, Go changing the way you think about the adult discipleship ministry of your church?

What do you plan to do in the next six months in the groups that you influence? What do you plan to do to provide more balance in your own spiritual life?

Keep the Conversations Going

1. Evaluate your ministries, just as Ken's church did (Getting Started, pp. 4-5), and learn about some new approaches.

All adult ministries should contribute to making disciples. Worship experiences, Sunday School, ministry opportunities, and fellowship all can be used to guide people to be transformed into Christlikeness.

The most effective disciple-making ministries are intentionally balanced so believers can grow through a variety of means. Open groups are most often found in Sunday School, with the Bible as the teaching content. Closed groups can meet at times convenient to participants and topics relate to the needs of the group, as Allen discovered (Grow, pp. 23-24). Resources are carefully and strategically planned for study. For adults, a balance is desired.

The Great Commission tells us, "Go, therefore, and make disciples of all nations, baptizing them in the name of the Father and of the Son and of the Holy Spirit, teaching them to observe everything I have commanded you" (Matt. 28:19-20). Christ's directions are quite plain: make disciples. While the directive is clear, the definition may not necessarily be. What really is the disciple-making ministry of the church? Disciple-making, as shown in the diagram on the following page, guides people to be transformed into Christlikeness so they think and act like Christ.

For more information about these vital dynamics of adult ministry and discipleship, go to *www.lifeway.com* and search "adult strategy." Currently these pages provide Webcourses on Connect, Grow, Serve, Go and LifeSpan Spiritual Development (*www.lifeway.com/lifespan*). New items, including downloads related to this resource, are frequently added.

For a fee, leaders can take the Spiritual Formation Inventory and receive an assessment. This evaluation may be accessed at *www.lifeway.com* by searching "Spiritual Formation Inventory."

Disciple Making Process

Disciple-making guides people to be transformed
in Christlikeness so they think and act like Christ.

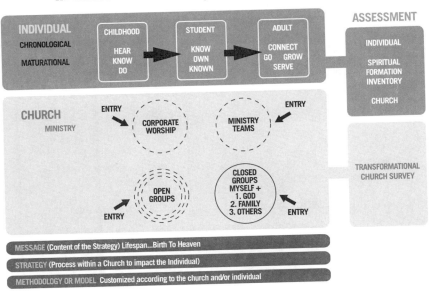

2. Try something new.

Look for success as you develop and begin to implement a balanced plan. Intentionally add a new group if one is needed and would contribute to the balance you need.

Make some initial notes in this space and talk with key members and leaders. Then watch to see whether your new intentionality gives focus, balance, and—most importantly—results.

3. See how Connect, Grow, Serve, Go fits into the big picture with other age groups.

Childhood and student ministries are built around age-appropriate strategies, goals, and resources, too—all of which contribute to adults hearing, responding to, and living out the gospel. As a result, leaders and parents can help lay important foundations for preschoolers, children, and students.

Preschool and children's resources and strategy are built around the Levels of Biblical Learning ministry tool and the theme Hear, Know, Do. KNOWN, a strategy for student development, helps students know Christ, own their faith, and make their faith known. And adults focus on creating fully mature Christians using Connect, Grow, Serve, Go. For more information, please visit *www.lifeway.com/lifespan*.

Talk with your preschool, children's, and student leaders to find ways to coordinate efforts. Working as a team helps the church maximize its impact, including to families and homes.

4. Consider whether a Bible study on Connect, Grow, Serve, Go would benefit your groups.

Visit *www.lifeway.com/adultstrategy* for four lessons. These free downloads can help churches strengthen their process of making disciples, particularly through Sunday School and small groups. Lessons will help individuals further understand their responsibilities as a disciple. Consider using lessons in a variety of ways, including to:
—Teach a general class on discipleship.
—Influence new member or new believer training.
—Train Sunday School leaders.
—Teach from the pulpit.
—Pull out specific lessons for a needs-based emphasis, such as a focus on service.

5. Over time, keep track of the various icons that categorize resources you use with adults.

As your adult ministry provides a consistent, balanced (there's that word *balance* again) offering of Connect, Grow, Serve, and Go resources, observe how adults are receiving the whole counsel of God and reflecting a healthy, balanced spiritual life.

To learn more about how your resources can help you create a Connect, Grow, Serve, Go plan, visit *www.lifeway.com/curriculumguide.* For ways undated studies can contribute to that plan, search *www.lifeway.com* for discipleship resources and look under the appropriate Connect, Grow, Serve, Go category for possible solutions.

What resources does your church use to help families face the myriad of life's challenges? Could great family magazines be part of your church's solution? What other help would you add?

As Jesus looked over the city of Jerusalem, He was moved to tears (Luke 19:41). Who did He see that moved Him so deeply? Did He see the people who, even then, were plotting to kill Him? Did He see the lame? What about the rich?

He saw them all and was moved with compassion by their condition. He saw them as lost and needing God's salvation. He knew they had ended up on the wrong path and couldn't turn around on their own. He could see their future and feel their pain. He saw us.

This was the love that motivated Jesus to leave His place in heaven, to endure the pain of the cross, all for you and me.

Love causes a person to do things that make no sense to others. That's just the way true love is. It is His kind of love that motivates us when, as individuals, groups, and churches, we truly Connect, Grow, Serve, Go.

---

1. Dan Olivia, "Church Corner: Keeping tabs on humans and our foibles must be like herding cats" [online], 16 November 2009 [cited 15 January 2010]. Available from the Internet: www.pnwlocalnews.com.